Fellowship Of The Lord's Supper

Robert L. Robinson Ph.D.

Copyright © 2011 by Robert L. Robinson
Robert Robinson Ministries
PO Box 10106
Cranston, RI 02910

Visit our website at
www.robertrobinsonministries.org

*This book is written and dedicated to the memory of
my closest and dearest friend
Apostle Lowell White
rest in Him, miss you much
Robby*

Foreword

How did I do a study on the subject of communion? This teaching is the result of a series of bad events while attempting to return home from one of my meetings. I had preached at my dear cousin Bishop Michael Brown's church in Fort Pierce Florida and after traveling and ministering for over twenty years, I suffered the worst time trying to get home from Ft. Pierce Florida; it was an event to say the least. I got up early that morning in Ft. Pierce at about 3:00am to drive back to West Palm Beach to catch my 6:30am flight which would have gotten me home in time for Sunday morning service at House of Manna Ministries. My flight was leaving out of West Palm Beach because Fort Pierce doesn't have an airport. After arriving at the airport, I found out that my Delta flight (flying standby) was full and I kept getting bumped. So, being that I wouldn't be able to get home until that Wednesday, I had to do the next best thing, which was to fly out of Tampa. So, using my iPad (thank the Lord) I booked a flight leaving out of Tampa on Monday and at the time of the situation, it was Sunday. After booking my flight, I went to the area that provides transportation and asked them if there was a shuttle that went to Tampa, (I thought Tampa was about 20-30 miles away). The nice gentleman looked at me and said, "I can get you to Tampa but it would cost about $500." I didn't know Tampa was 200 miles away. So he recommended that I catch a train from West Palm Beach to Tampa. After waiting at the train station for five hours, I was able to board the train for Tampa and after the three-hour train ride I finally arrived in Tampa. I had to take a taxi from Tampa railroad station to the hotel located at the airport and thank the Lord I had my phone on, because the taxi driver, bless his heart, was going to take me a roundabout way. Well, when I finally arrived at my hotel in Tampa, of course, I was frustrated, tired, lonely, hungry and most importantly homesick because for some reason I really wanted to be home in my own church on that Sunday morning, but it just didn't work out.

After I relaxed and talked with Glenda to let her know I was alright, the strangest thought came to my mind and now I believe it was the Holy Spirit. The thought of communion just began to keep ringing in my heart and in my spiritual ears. I said to myself, "wow" it's a subject that I don't hear much about anymore. The church that I pastor, House of Manna Ministries, do celebrate the Lord's Supper and again I said to myself "is there much information that helps many to understand its importance?" So being the writer that the Lord has blessed me to be, I knew what was coming next, the Lord said, "Robby, I want you to write a book about the importance of celebrating the Lord's Supper," and I said to the Holy Spirit, "not a problem I pray that you release the revelation the people will need."

I began to teach on communion in our local church and I was caught off guard by the response of the teaching. Many were set free in their minds because of the understanding they received. The communion teaching has changed everyone's understanding and the celebration services are powerful. This is how I ended up writing this book, Fellowship of the Lord's Supper.

Table of Contents

Fellowship of the Lord's Supper is based upon a teaching and serves as a clear biblical and basic understanding of the importance of communion. It seeks to restore the confidence in the believer and to also teach that the celebration of communion is not meant to be so sanctimonious that many fear to partake in it. All believers are to celebrate the Lord's Supper.

There are many myths concerning the Lord's Supper such as one should not eat breakfast prior to taking the Lord's Supper, another myth is one should live the 100% perfect lifestyle prior to celebrating communion because you have to be worthy to take it. Believers, communion was not intended to bring fear, communion is supposed to bring liberty! Another myth is one being unworthy. Paul does not use the word unworthy in 1 Corinthians 11:27, 29, he uses the word "unworthily" which is a huge difference.

Myths that hinder the believer from celebrating the Lord's Supper is a trick of the enemy. Celebrating the Lord's Supper shows our deliverance, what is deliverance? Deliverance is the defeat of the enemy. The enemy was exposed and his works destroyed at Calvary and that defeat is still alive and powerful today, so we celebrate that defeat over the enemy when we celebrate the Lord's Supper.

Fellowship of the Lord's Supper empowers the believer, it reminds the believer of what Christ Jesus did, and it gives continuous life to the believer. As you read, be taught, truly study and be strengthened by the Holy Spirit. May your knowledge and wisdom grow because of Him, may He be glorified in all that we celebrate in Him, and may the enemy be horrified at the revelation of this teaching.

Shalom,

R.L. Robinson

Communion can actually be seen as early as the Old Testament. It began when the Israelites were in Egypt and that celebration was known as Passover. Although the Passover is mentioned numerous times in the Bible, the most important description is found in Exodus 12. That account not only tells the story of what happened on the night of the first Passover but also gives detailed instructions for how the people of Israel were supposed to keep the Passover also known as the Feast.

In my book entitled The Feasts of the Lord I state the following, "How did the Feasts begin? It started with Moses and the Hebrews when they were serving as slaves to Egypt under a Pharaoh. The cries of the Children had come up before the Lord so He rose up a deliverer named Moses to bring the Children out of Egypt. The first Passover transpired nearly 3500 years ago when the Hebrew's were captives in Egypt. The Lord said to Moses in Exodus 12:1-2 that this month shall be to you the beginning of months and that it would be the first month of the year to Moses. This meant that God was changing the calendar by initiating a new one. The month that they were in at that time would be called the first month or the month of Aviv (the name was later changed to Nisan). Hebraically this particular calendar became known as the Sacred or Religious calendar. The month of

Aviv became the first month on the Hebrew (sacred) calendar.

On the 10th day of the month of Aviv the Lord instructed Moses to have each family take a lamb which was to be without spot or blemish and was to be kept until the 14th day of Aviv. The Lamb was prepared by being killed and according to history the lamb was to be displayed for all to see. "The lamb was to be cooked on a cross of pomegranate sticks, its head was to be upright and the upper limbs were tied outspread horizontally. Its feet were tied at the bottom; the intestines were removed and wrapped around the head in what was known as the Crown of salvation ." The blood from the lamb was caught in a basin and hyssop (a strong wiry plant whose bunches of flowers and leaves were good at absorbing liquid and was used sought of like a brush), was dipped into the basin and then the blood was spread on all four sides of the doorpost, in essence they made the sign of the cross over their homes.

On the 14th day, the lamb was to be killed in the evening or *bain haarbayim*, which means "between the evenings" or precisely at 3:00 PM. The lamb was to be killed at 3:00 PM, roasted then eaten at 6:00 PM and was to be eaten with unleavened bread and bitter herbs and nothing from the lamb was to be leftover.

From that night onward, all the way to the time of Jesus (and beyond), the Passover would be celebrated each spring as a "day of remembrance," an ordinance that was to be carried out "forever" according to Exodus 12:14. The Book of Exodus not only tells the history of what happened on Passover night but also lays out the sacrificial ritual that was to be carried out by the Jewish people on that first night and for all time.

Many years has passed since the first celebration of the Passover Feast and todays celebration of the Lord's Supper. From Exodus of Egypt through the times of Jesus, the Jewish Passover has developed changes. In the first celebration of Passover when they were in Egypt, the lamb was slain and the blood was placed on the doorposts of the home, that order is not practiced anymore. The location of the Passover celebration has changed. In the first celebration of the Passover the lambs were sacrificed, eaten in the homes of the Israelites while in they were in Egypt. At the time of the celebration of the Passover during the time of Jesus, the lambs were sacrificed in the Temple and eaten in the city of Jerusalem. Today among Jews, Passover is celebrated in the home.

During the time of the first Passover, the Israelite father was to offer sacrifice on behalf of his family but at the time of Jesus, only the Levitical Priests could pour out the blood of the lambs on the altar at the Jerusalem Temple for the Passover. At the time in Jesus' day only the lamb could lawfully be offered in one place which was the Temple of Jerusalem.

In 1 Corinthians 5:7, Paul refers to Christ as our Passover and that Passover is sacrificed for us. What is meant by the word Passover? The word Passover is the Greek word *pascha* (pas'-khah), which denotes the meal, the day, the festival or the special sacrifices connected with Passover. The Hebrew word for Passover is pe-sahh which means, "The day of deliverance from Egypt," it also means, "to remember this day the Lamb that is sacrificed." One writer says, "Jesus' sacrifice was the first Eucharist that transformed Jesus' death from an execution to an offering." It was at that time that Jesus' body was given to be broken and His blood was to be poured out upon the altar. Jesus is our Passover, our deliverance from Egypt.

> *1Cor. 11:24-25*
> *And when he had given thanks, he brake it, and said, Take, eat: this is my body, which is broken for you: this do in re-membrance of me. After the same manner also he took the cup, when he had supped, saying, This cup is the new testament in my blood: this do ye, as oft as ye drink it, in remembrance of me.*

What is communion? In 1 Corinthians 11:20 Paul refers to communion as the Lord's Supper, Luke 24:35 and Acts 2:42; 20:7 communion is

Robert L. Robinson Ph.D.

referred to as the breaking of bread, in 1 Corinthians 10:21, Paul refers to communion as the Lord's Table and in 1 Corinthians 10:16-17 Paul refers to the cup and the bread as a participation or communion in the body and blood of Christ.

> *1Cor. 10:20*
> *But I say, that the things which the Gentiles sacrifice, they sacrifice to devils, and not to God: and I would not that ye should have fellowship with devils.*

The word fellowship in 1 Corinthians 10:20 is the Greek word *koinonos* (koy-no-nos') which denotes, fellowship, participation in, or communion. The word *koinonos* better known as *koinonia* denotes fellowship or communion with a common purpose or identity; it means more than just a common association such as in a human activity such as a sports team, it is a fellowship that connects and identifies the believer for a common purpose. Another word used in association with communion is the word *Eucharist* that comes from the Greek by way of Latin, and means "thanksgiving." It is used in three ways: first, to refer to the real presence of Christ; second, to refer to Christ's continuing action as High Priest (He "gave thanks" at the Last Supper, which began the consecration of the bread and wine); and third, to refer to the Sacrament of Holy Communion itself.

8

What is communion? Communion is the celebration and the remembering of and giving thanks to the Lord Jesus for He being our sacrifice and through His sacrifice gives us the believer redemption. Communion is the celebration of the Lord's Supper, the breaking of bread, participation in the body and blood of Christ. Communion is the koinonia, it is the celebration of fellowship with one another reminding us all of our common purpose and identity, our purpose is Christ and we are identified with Him. Communion is the Eucharist, the celebration of thanksgiving.

Luke 15:20
And he arose, and came to his father. But when he was yet a great way off, his father saw him, and had compassion, and ran, and fell on his neck, and kissed him.

Communion reveals many things to the believer. In Luke 15-20, we learn of the story of the prodigal son. He was a young man and while working for his father wanted to leave so he asked his father for his portion. The father gave the young son his portion and the son left his father's house and went on his own. While on his own the bible reads that the young man spent his entire portion on riotous living and eventually ended up having to work in a field feeding the swine. The son had grown to such of a low estate that he ended up eating the same food as the swine but then he came to himself and said, "I will arise and go to my father." In Luke 15:20, upon returning, the father saw his son returning but he was a great way off. His father saw him and went to him, he ran, fell on his neck and kissed his son. There is a beautiful picture of communion and what communion reveals.

The son left his father and though his son made bad decisions, he was able to return to his father he welcomed him with open arms. The

Robert L. Robinson Ph.D.

father welcoming the son means that the father was not holding anything against the son and has forgiven him. The kiss represents all is forgiven. Communion reveals the forgiveness of the Heavenly Father; He's not holding anything against us and all has been forgiven. Forgiveness is a gift given not a gift earned and it is not given because of one's social status. Forgiveness is a gift from God and it is revealed in the celebration of the Lord's Supper, our forgiveness is seen in the celebration of communion.

Not only does communion reveal the forgiveness from our Father, but it also reveals the acceptance of our Father. Note what the father said when his son returned in Luke 15:23, "And bring hither the fatted calf, and kill it; and let us eat, and be merry." The word merry is the Greek word *euphraino* (yoo-frah'ee-no), which means, "in a good frame of mind, rejoice." It became a celebration which put those who were celebrating into a good frame of mind which caused them to rejoice. Why did they make merry or become in a good frame of mind? They were happy because the prodigal son returned home, the guilt of his past actions were not held against him by his father. Communion reveals the Father's acceptance of you. The prodigal son was a wayward child that returned and was accepted. In biblical times when a person is invited to eat by another it meant that the person invited was accepted.

Communion reveals the acceptance from the Father to His wayward son, his children; it's the Father's acceptance of the believer.

> *Luke 24:30-31*
> *And it came to pass, as he sat at meat with them, he took bread, and blessed it, and brake, and gave to them. (31) their eyes were opened, and they knew him; and he vanished out of their sight.*

There is another point to be made as to what communion reveals. In Luke 24 there were two men who were on their way to a village called Emmaus and as they were walking they talked of what had transpired with the crucifixion of Jesus that happened a few days prior. While they were talking, Jesus drew near to them but the two men did not recognize him then Jesus asked what they were talking about that was keeping them so miserable.

The one named Cleopas answered and said, *"are you a stranger in Jerusalem and do not know what happened these past days?"* Jesus answered, "What change?" The men were very upset over what had taken place and so the Cleopas begins to talk about Jesus of Nazareth who was a mighty prophet before God and the people and how the chief priest condemned Jesus to death and was crucified. Cleopas went on to say that they had hoped that Jesus would redeem Israel.

At that time it had been three days since the crucifixion has transpired. Jesus in the course of the conversation makes this statement, "O fools, and slow of heart to believe all that the prophets have spoken: Ought not Christ to have suffered these things, and to enter into his glory? And beginning at Moses and all the prophets, he expounded unto them in all the scriptures the things concerning himself." About that time the three of them came close to the village and the two men asked Jesus to stay with them because it was evening, so Jesus went in and stayed with them. Jesus sat at meat with the two men when he then took the bread and blessed it, broke it and gave it to the two men. It was at that time that the eyes of the two men were opened. Note, their eyes came open when Jesus took the bread and blessed it and broke it and gave it. That's communion celebrated and in that celebration the two men's eyes were opened and they saw Jesus. What does communion reveal? Communion reveals the very presence of Jesus.

1 Corinthians 13:1-3
Though I speak with the tongues of men and of angels, and have not charity, I am become as sounding brass, or a tinkling cymbal. (2) And though I have the gift of prophecy, and understand all myster ies, and all knowledge; and though I have

all faith, so that I could remove moun-
tains, and have not charity, I am nothing.

Another revelation to be learned in communion is noted in 1 Corinthians 13:3. Note that Paul begins in verse 1 by saying though he speaks with the tongues of man and angels but has not love, he says he's as a sounding brass and tinkling cymbal which means he just makes a lot of noise. Paul goes on to say that if he has the give of prophecy and understands all mysteries and all knowledge and have all faith to move mountains but has no love he is nothing. Paul then says in verse 3 that though he bestows all of his goods to feed the poor and though he gives his body to be burned and have not charity it profiteth him nothing. Let's look at verse 3 very closely. The word burned comes into question. The word burned in the Greek is *kaio* (kah'-yo), which means, "to set on fire, to kindle, consume." However, there is some confusion over this word because other manuscripts give the word to mean, "boast." The New English Translation (NET) uses the word boast. Paul was saying though I give all my goods to feed the poor and though I give my body to boast and have not charity or love it profiteth me nothing. We do not shine or boast when we serve one another, we serve one another because we love one another and communion reveals our love for one another for love is the foundation of our fellowship

Communion reveals our Heavenly Fathers love, forgiveness and acceptance of us all. The fellowship of the Lord's Supper also reveals the very presence of Jesus and finally communion and fellowship reveals our love for one another, we are connected to each other through communion.

In this chapter we shall look at two important elements of the celebration of the Lord's Supper, the bread and the wine. We see the Lords Supper practiced in the Old Testament.

> *Genesis 14:18-19*
> *And Melchizedek king of Salem brought forth bread and wine: and he was the priest of the most high God. (19) And he blessed him, and said, Blessed be Abram of the most high God, possessor of heaven and earth:*

In Genesis 14, Abram returned from battle and brought back all the spoils or goods along with Lot. Upon returning in verse 18 Melchizedek king of Salem brought forth bread and wine. Melchizedek was a priest of the most high God. This served as a type of communion and fellowship. Abram came from battle and what does a person need after a battle? One needs restoration, the bread and wine restored Abram and the bread restores the believer.

> *Exodus 16:14-15*
> *And when the dew that lay was gone up, behold, upon the face of the wilderness there lay a small round thing, as small as the hoar frost on the ground. (15) And*

Robert L. Robinson Ph.D.

> *when the children of Israel saw it, they said one to another, It is manna: for they wist not what it was. And Moses said unto them, this is the bread which the Lord hath given you to eat.*

Let us look at manna. In Exodus chapter 16, the children of Israel after being in the desert for just a short time, began to murmur and complain. They felt as though they were better of remaining in Egypt because though they were under an oppressor at least they had something to eat. So, the Lord told Moses that He would rain down "bread from heaven." When the bread was released, the children of Israel called it manna, which in the Hebrew is pronounced man and basically means, "what is this?" The people were instructed to gather a day's portion early in the morning every day except for the Sabbath. When it was Sabbath they would gather enough the day prior to Sabbath to hold them over after the Sabbath and if they attempted to gather more the manna would spoil. They were instructed to gather the manna before the sun became so hot as to melt it.

The manna in the desert was no ordinary bread. It was miraculous "bread from heaven," given directly by God to his people for them to eat. The manna strengthened the children of Israel as they traveled through the wilderness in the desert.

Exodus 24:9-11   Then went up Moses, and Aaron, Nadab, and Abihu, and seventy of the elders of Israel: (10)   And they saw the God of Israel: and there was under his feet as it were a paved work of a sapphire stone, and as it were the body of heaven in his clearness.   (11)   And upon the nobles of the children of Israel he laid not his hand: also they saw God, and did eat and drink.

In Exodus 24, Moses, Joshua, Aaron and his sons and the seventy elders from Israel then proceeded to Mt. Sinai. When they got there they saw the God of Israel. The word saw is the Hebrew word *ra'ah* (raw-aw') which mainly means, "to behold." Beheld is a word that is usually connected with vision, so, the entourage beheld the God is Israel in a vision. The Lord walked on a pavement that was the color of sapphire which was a crystal clear blue glass. All who were with Moses bowed to the Lord and worshipped him afar, but close enough to see what He was walking on. They then did eat and drink. The eating and drinking served as a confirming covenant meal (Ex. 18:22, Gen. 31:46,54) and served as a type of communion, which is a reminder of the covenant relationship between two parties. This meal signified that all those who were on the mountain were in agreement with what the Lord was going to do.

Hebrews 9:2
For there was a tabernacle made; the first,

wherein was the candlestick, and the table, and the Shewbread; which is called the sanctuary.

There were three major objects in the Tabernacle of Moses, the Ark of the Covenant, the golden lamp stand also known as the Menorah and the table of Shewbread, also known as the Bread of the Presence. Hebrews 9:2 speaks of what the sanctuary area of the Tabernacle consisted of, the seven-branded candlestick, the table or altar of incense and the table of Shewbread. The table of Shewbread was also known as the "Bread of the Presence" and the Hebrew expression is "Bread of the Face." It means the bread laid before God in His presence, it is also rendered as the Bread of the Face of God. The twelve loaves, which were two piles of six loaves in each, represented the twelve tribes, but was also a figure of He who was to come, which was Christ. Jesus is referred to in scripture as the bread of life (John 6:35). He is also the bread that came from heaven (John 6:33) the living bread (John 6:51). If we eat of the Bread of Life and drink His blood then we have eternal life (John 6:54).

Hebrews 9:4 speaks of the Golden Pot of Manna being in the Ark of the Covenant. The Golden Pot of Manna speaks of Jesus Christ, gold denotes His divine nature, and bread denotes His keeping and restoring power

John 6:53-56
Then Jesus said unto them, Verily, verily,
I say unto you, Except ye eat the flesh of
the Son of man, and drink his blood, ye
have no life in you. Whoso eateth my
flesh, and drinketh my blood, hath eternal
life; and I will raise him up at the last
day. [55] For my flesh is meat indeed,
and my blood is drink indeed. [56] He
that eateth my flesh, and drinketh my
blood, dwelleth in me, and I in him.

In John 6:53, Jesus said, "Then Jesus said unto them, verily, verily, I say unto you, except ye eat the flesh of the Son of man, and drink his blood, ye have no life in you." Note that Jesus was speaking at that time to Jewish listeners in the synagogue and when He uttered those words many of the Jewish followers were offended, the bible reads that many of his disciples said, "This is a hard saying who can hear it?" They were offended and many no longer walked with Jesus. They were offended because they lacked revelation and faith in what Jesus was teaching at that time. The communion or Eucharist denotes two very important elements, the bread and the wine, the bread also referred to as the flesh denotes the body of Christ while the wine denotes the blood of Christ.

Jesus in John 6:55 refers to flesh which denotes His body and continues to say that he that eats His flesh and drinks His blood has fellowship with me and I in him. That is in connection with Jesus' death on the cross.

The bread denotes the very presence of Jesus and just as God had been the sign of the everlasting covenant, now communion is the perpetual sign of the new covenant sealed in the blood of Christ. The Bread of the Presence was the bread of the Face of God, so now communion would be the Bread of the face of Christ. According to the writings of Saint Cyril of Jerusalem who was a native of the Holy Land and bishop of the Church in Jerusalem in the fourth century AD, he explains the mystery of the Bread of the Presence by saying "In the Old Testament also there was the Bread of the Presence; but this, as it belonged to the Old Testament, has come to an end but in the New Testament there is bread of heaven and a cup of salvation, sanctifying soul and body... Consider therefore the bread and the wine not as bare elements, for they are, according to the Lord's declaration, the body and blood of Christ; for even though sense suggests this to you, yet let faith establish you. Judge not the matter from the taste, but from faith be fully assured without misgiving, that body and blood of Christ have been vouchsafed to you. "

What about the wine? There are some major areas in the scripture, which gives clear meaning and relevance of the blood. In Exodus 12:23 it was the blood of the lamb that saved the Hebrews in the Passover. The lamb was cut from the neck down and the blood was caught in a basin which was a ditch dug in front of the doorways to avoid flooding. Hyssop (a strong wiry plant whose bunches of flowers and leaves were good at absorbing liquid and was used sought of like a brush) was dipped into the basin and then the blood was spread on all four sides of the doorpost, in essence they made the sign of the cross over their homes.

The blood also secured them causing the Hebrews to Passover or Pass-over. The Hebrew word Passover is actually connected with an Egypt word pesh which means, "to spread wings over" in order to protect. So the Passover caused the Lord not only to pass through the land but to also protect those who were covered in the blood.

In the first Passover the lamb was killed, throat was slit, blood was caught in the basin, and then the lamb itself was roasted then eaten with bitter herbs and unleavened bread. The unleavened bread in Hebrew is matzah. It denoted how the Israelites had to bake the bread in haste when they left Egypt; there was no time to allow the bread to rise. The bitter herbs commemorated the sufferings sustained while the children of Israel were in Egypt. The Lamb could not be eaten raw or boiled or cut into pieces. It was spitted with wooden rods and roasted over a fire and then eaten that very same night.

Note the connection of the blood and the bread. The blood denotes the blood of Jesus; the bread denotes the body of Jesus! Communion is the breaking of bread (His Body), the drinking of His blood which unites the believer as one in Christ Jesus.

This is a question that is asked by many because there have been many misconceptions about the Lord's Supper. Before we look at who is worthy to take communion, let's look at how often communion should be celebrated. There is no detailed information concerning how often communion should be celebrated in the scriptures. However, it is often celebrated.

In Acts 2, the disciples devoted themselves to "breaking of bread." In Acts 20:7 they came to Troas where they abode for seven days and on the first day of the week the disciples came together and broke bread. The saints at Corinth gathered regularly to observe the Lord's Supper (1 Cor. 11:18). So, as we see, many times throughout the New Testament, they met on a weekly basis to celebrate the Lord's Supper.

During the Time of Reformation, Calvin in his treatise states, "Though we have no express command defining the time and the day, it should be enough for us to know that the intention of our Lord is that we use it often; otherwise we shall not know well the benefits which it offers " There is no set time to celebrate the Lord's Supper however it is important that we do celebrate it, in essence we cannot celebrate the Lord's Supper enough!

1 Corinthians 11:27-30
*Wherefore whosoever shall eat this bread,
and drink this cup of the Lord, unworthily, shall be guilty of the body and blood of
the Lord. (28) But let a man examine
himself, and so let him eat of that bread,
and drink of that cup. (29) For he that
eateth and drinketh unworthily, eateth
and drinketh damnation to himself, not
discerning the Lord's body. (30) For this
cause many are weak and sickly among
you, and many sleep.*

Now, who is worthy to take communion?
Well let me begin by reminding many of you,
including myself, of the excuses that we used even
I before I came into the truth. I would take communion but I am unworthy and don't expose
myself to condemnation so must wait until the next
time and hopefully I will be worthy and better
prepared to celebrate the Lords Supper. Does that
sound familiar? It is because many of you including myself didn't really understand what Paul was
saying in 1 Corinthians. So let's look at where the
confusion started.

The confusion started with the word "unworthily." Most including myself interpreted the
word unworthily with the word unworthy and
because of this felt as though they were unworthy
in regards to their personal qualifications and
being unfit to celebrate the Lord's Supper. The

word unworthily does not relate to your qualifications because none are qualified but it's only through the blood of Jesus that has made us qualified to celebrate the Lord's Supper. Unworthily refers to how we observe the ordinance of the Lords Supper, how you approach the Lord's Supper. The word unworthily is the Greek word anaxios which means, "in an unworthy or improper manner" or "in a manner unsuitable to the purposes for which it was designed or instituted." It has nothing to do with how you dress, it has to do with how you approach the Lord, you must approach the Lord in a manner suitable to the purpose for which it was created for, and it is one's observance of the Lord's Supper that can get an individual in trouble.

How do we observe the Lord's Supper? We observe the Lord's Supper by observing that He is our redeemer, we are unfit but He makes us fit, we were lost without our Savoir, His blood has given us righteousness or made us right with God and because of this we are able to stand before Him and celebrate his death burial and resurrection. It's by the blood of Jesus that we are able to stand in the presence of a Holy Father and be declared righteous before Him. Well, what about the sin issue that I commit? When you commit sin, you don't wait until you get to the Lord's Table to get forgiveness, you get forgiveness when you commit it!

The scripture reads, "Whosoever shall eat this bread, and drink this cup of the Lord, unworthily, shall be guilty of the body and blood of the Lord." The word guilty is the Greek word enochoi which means "obnoxious to punishment for personal crime." It actually denotes one who is liable to, or is in danger of a penalty or punishment because of one's actions." It is the exposure to punishment because of a crime. Another writer puts it this way, "Shall be guilty of a misuse of the body and blood of the Lord." So what can one be guilty of in celebrating the Lord's Supper? One can be guilty of not discerning the Lord's body; it's how one approaches the celebration that is important.

What does discerning the Lord's body mean? The word discerning is the Greek word diakrino (dee-ak-ree'-no) which means, to separate thoroughly or to make a distinction." You discern the Lord's body by judging it, seeing what you need, seeing his body on Calvary for your deliverance. You discern the Lord's body by examining it as well as examining yourself. You examine his body for the healing and the deliverance of you. Know what you want from the Lord; know what His body represents and what his death burial and resurrection does for you. And this is the reason or cause why many are weak and sickly among us, and many sleep because they did not discern the

Lord's body, they did not approach the body of the Lord Jesus to get what they needed.

Who is worthy to take communion? None of us are worthy on our own, however Jesus has made us worthy. Now as you approach the Lord's Table, discern His body. Look at the body and see what He died for, discern it and note the benefits you as a believer have because of His body and blood. Healing, deliverance and life is in His body and in His blood, now as you take eat and drink, take what you need from Him. Who is worthy to partake of communion? Those whom the Lord has made free, those who know how to discern the Lord's Body.

What does communion actually do for all those who partake in the Lord's Supper? We will begin by looking at Genesis 2:7, noting some truths there. Genesis 2:7 reads, "And the Lord God formed man of the dust of the ground, and breathed into his nostrils the breath of life; and man became a living soul." Notice the scripture says that the Lord God formed man. The word formed is the Hebrew word yatsar (yaw-tsar') which gives the idea of one squeezing or molding someone into shape. It denotes one such as a potter who has determined a form for something though that something is clay in, in this case, an individual and the potter has made that form by squeezing that form into shape. The Lord formed you and now the Lord must breathe into you. What does the Lord God breathe into you? He breathes life. Let's look at the word life. The word Life is the Hebrew word chay (khah'ee) and the verbal root of chay is chayah. Chayah is generally translated as "living" or "quickened." In that we understand that man's life came from the breath or Spirit of God so, life in this sense means that which is living or quickened by the Spirit of God. God formed or squeezed into shape man (you the believer) and breathed into you life which made you living or quickened you, by quicken I mean He caused you to come alive.

Deuteronomy 32:46-47
*And he said unto them, set your hearts
un to all the words which I testify among
you this day, which ye shall command
your children to observe to do, all the
words of this law. (47) For it is not a
vain thing for you; because it is your life:
and through this thing ye shall prolong
your days in the land, whither ye go over
Jordan to possess it.*

Another form of the word life in the scriptures is noted in Deuteronomy 32:46-47, it speaks
of the Lord commanding the children to observe to
do all the words of this law because it is your life!
Life here in Deuteronomy relates to one keeping
laws, precepts ordinances, statues, words and
teachings of the Lord. With this understanding of
the word life we come to understand that life also
denotes the believer observing and obeying the
Word, it gives life to the believer, "it is your life."

Another meaning for the word life is noted
in the Hebrew Lexicon, which describes an empty
stomach, causing an individual to be famished, and
weak but when filled it is revived." So also denotes a reviving or a filling of that which is empty.
Psalms 119:144 reads "The righteousness of thy
testimonies is everlasting: give me understanding,
and I shall live." The Spirit of God breathed upon
us and gave us life, we were empty but then filled
because He breathed life and we are continuously

given life because of the observing of His word, Psalms 119: 28 reads "strengthen thou me according to thy word." Isaiah 8:20, "To the law and to the testimony: if they speak not according to this word, it is because there is no light in them." If they speak not according to this word, there is no light or life in them.

> *John 1:1*
> *In the beginning was the Word, and the Word was with God, and the Word was God.*

Jesus is the Word of God; He is not just concepts and thoughts but the actual Word of God in the flesh. According to Orthodox Jewish beliefs, when the scriptures read that the Word of God came to Jeremiah or Moses it is believed that God himself came to them and it is clear that the New Testament teaches that the words of God that was established in the Old Testament took upon flesh and dwelt among us, so Jesus is the actual word of God both literally and figuratively. Jesus is the Word of God and He is also Bread.

The Shewbread in the tabernacle sat in the sanctuary and was to be eaten by the priests on the seventh day while functioning in the sanctuary in order to strengthen him while performing his duties. Shewbread was called the Bread of the Presence," or "Bread of the Face" which meant "the bread laid before God in His presence." The

Shewbread denotes life, Jesus is "The Bread of Life" (John 6:35), and as the priests ate the bread while in the sanctuary so must we the believer eat the bread for as we eat the bread we impart into our being more life. The table of Shewbread is Christ the Bread and since Christ is the bread it is important that we the believer constantly eat Christ, for He is the manna or the sustaining power of the believer. The Bread is the Life of God.

> *John 10:10*
> *The thief cometh not, but for to steal, and*
> *to kill, and to destroy: I am come that*
> *they might have life, and that they might*
> *have it more abundantly.*

John 10:10 reads that Jesus came to give us life and to give it more abundantly. The Greek word for life in John 10:10 is *zoe* (dzo-ay') which means "living" and refers to a quality that distinguishes a vital and functional being from a dead body." How does Jesus do give life? Jesus gives life through the power of His words that are put into action in the life of the believer. Remember now, the bread denotes Life of God and the Life of God going into you. When Jesus said He comes that we may have life it means that the power of His words when put into action will give us life. The bread is a constant reminder and restorer of the Life and Power of God and His Word!

The Lord God formed you and breathed into you, life which quickened you. That life is constantly given through His Word by observing, believing, and walking in the Word, by keeping His statutes and teachings. We also noted that Jesus is the Word, the literal Word, and Jesus is the Bread, Jesus is the Life, the Word and Jesus is the Life giver, He gives life. What does communion give? Communion then gives life.

How does communion give life? Each individual that is formed is formed differently. However, when Father God formed you, He fixed you to need breath! Yes, the Father has made it so that you would always need His breath. His breath is His life, His life is His Word, and His Word is His bread! When the Children of Israel were in the wilderness they ate manna, every morning as they were instructed to gather it in the morning. Jesus said in Matthew 6:11 "give us this day our daily bread" which serves as a daily request from the believer for bread, that bread is needed both naturally and spiritually, a bread for the natural man and a bread for the spirit man. You constantly need life! John 6:53 reads "Except ye eat the flesh of the Son of man, and drink his blood, ye have no life in you."

Since Jesus the Word is the Bread and the giver of life then whenever we celebrate communion, we are ingesting His body, His Word and His life, and we are restored. So then communion gives the believer life! Many are battling with many things and the battle can weaken an individual so fellowship of the Lord's Supper is necessary in order for the believer to receive more life or should I say a restoring!

Why do many become weak and frail, why do many sleep? Because they dishonor the fellowship of Lord's Supper by celebrating it unworthily as previously stated. Everyone is unworthy to take communion but His blood makes the believer worthy, however many drink unworthily! It means that one does not honor the purpose of communion and you take it out of context, that's how you take it unworthily.

Communion gives Life, what does this mean it means that when I come to the Lord with a heavy heart, communion gives me life. If I have made a mistake and my head is low, the communion is what gives me life and restores me. Jesus died for your hang-ups and when an individual has a hang-up they are to bring those hang-ups to the Lord and get some restoration and life.

Sometime a false truth will come from a person who lacks spiritual insight and revelation. When an individual keeps a believer from celebrating the Lord's Supper that's a trick of the enemy, celebration of the Lord's Supper shows our deliverance, the enemy never likes for the remembrance of our deliverance to be celebrated because it reveals his defeat! The Bread and the Blood gives you life. You should not come to the Lords table with a heavy heart and leave with a heavy heart, its ok to come with a heavy heart but after ingesting his body and blood you leave the table uplifted, restored with life.

Accola, Louis, W Given for You "Reflections on
the Meaning of the Lord's Super."(Augsburg
Fortress: Minneapolis MN) 2007

Berthelson, Lou. Holiness For These Awesome
Days. (Shippensburg, PA: Destiny Image Publishers) 1991

Henry, Jim. In Remembrance of Me "A manual on
observing the Lord's Supper."(Broadman & Hol-
man Publishers: Nashville TN) 1998

Letham, Robert. The Lord's Supper "Eternal Word
in Broken Bread." (P&R Publishing: Phillipsburg
NJ) 2001

Marty, Martin. The Lord's Supper. (Augsburg
Press: MN) 1997

Pitre, Brant. Jesus and the Jewish Roots of the
Eucharist, "Unlocking the Secrets of the Last
Supper." (Doubleday: NY) 2011

Robinson, Robert L., "The Feasts of the Lord"
(Davedez Publishing: Cranston RI) 2009

Scott, Bradford. The Tanakh: The Dictionary of the
New Testament. (Children Are Forever Publishing: Littleton CO) 1997

Willimon, William. Sunday Dinner. (The Upper Room Publishers: Nashville TN) 1981

Can these bones live?
Gives specific prophetic instructions on how the ministry can be the ministry God are calling forth

The Authority of the Kingdom
The kingdom of God is here on earth within the believer and because of this position the believers must seek the kingdom in order to know more of and understand the kingdom.

How we got the Bible w/workbook
This book gives information concerning the history and makeup of the Bible. It deals with the many testing that were done in order to prove its authenticity. Comes with a workbook

Build Me a House
based on a teaching coming from the Old Testament book Ezra. This writing serves as a motivational prophetic Word to local churches encouraging them to complete the vision

Hebrews Chapter Nine "The Interpretation"
A teaching based on Hebrews chapter nine which deals with the Tabernacle of Moses.

The Ministry of the Tabernacle w/workbook
Book based on the Tabernacle of Moses

Build Me A House Correspondence Course
Build Me A House Correspondence Course is both a course and study guide based on Dr. Robinson's book entitled "Build Me A House." The course is based upon the book Ezra deals with church government and order.

A Sevenfold Purpose
A Sevenfold Purpose is the revealing of the will of God to His church as it pertains to alignment and order. The seven part plan is noted in the six days of creation leading into the seventh day.

Revelation, The Book w/workbook
Revelation, The Book is a commentary on the Book of Revelations which is the last prophetical book in the Bible

An Appointed Time
An Appointed Time is a set time, and this book prophetically deals with how the body of Christ must handle the appointed time allotted them.

Words Defined Prophetically
A book containing a selection of Biblical, Hebrew and Greek words detailing information concerning their meaning

Lessons I've Learned
This book is a compilation of bible studies taught by Dr. Robinson at a time when House of Manna Ministries in its inception stage

A Survey of the Old Testament w/ workbook
This book gives information pertaining to the Old Testament. A survey of the Old Testament deals with the History of Israel, their Kings, prophets, priests and ordinances. Book includes the workbook.

The Numbers Revealed
Throughout Scripture, numbers are used in order to reveal the hidden things of God. Through numbers God will release those things that are concealed.

The Necessity For Leadership
This book looks at leadership throughout the bible and deals with the importance of leaders aligning to God's order.

Fellowship Of The Lord's Supper

His Praise
In the King James Version (KJV) bible, the word praise is mentioned over one hundred and sixty times. However, in the original Hebrew, each praise words denotes a different meaning and action.

A Time to Work
This book is a word from the Lord that relates to a period when God will release an anointing for seed time and harvest

A Sevenfold Purpose Workbook
The Workbook to A Sevenfold Purpose

Jude's Letter
This is a writing based upon the book of Jude. In it you will find that Jude not only wrote to his generation, but his writings are prophetic which allowed for those writings to also speak to this generation.

The Four Anointing's
A prophetical writing on the four rivers noted in Genesis chapter 3

Be Free
Words of encouragement coming from both Pastor Glenda and Apostle Robinson

What are you Birthing?
Zacharias was an old man who was called and used by God to birth a son that was very important to the kingdom. You are not old, you just need to find your way.

Vision "The Pattern"
Vision is a book that goes into detail on how to manifest vision

Robert L. Robinson Ph.D.

Hebraic and Prophetic Interpretation of Biblical Words of the Old Testament
A compilation of word definitions and meanings from biblical words in the Old Testament.

Feasts of the Lord
The Feasts of the Lord is a prophetic look at the Old Testament Feast Days

36644021R00032

Made in the USA
Charleston, SC
09 December 2014